D1524219

A BRIEF HISTORY OF THE SHORT-LIVED

Chris Hutchinson

A Brief History of the Short-lived

NIGHTWOOD EDITIONS

2012

Nightwood Editions
P.O. Box 1779
Gibsons, BC VON 1VO
Canada
www.nightwoodeditions.com

TYPOGRAPHY & DESIGN: Carleton Wilson
COVER ART: Joseph Siddiqi, "Mad Love": oil on linen, 22 x 30 inches, 2011.

Nightwood Editions acknowledges financial support from the Government of Canada through the Canada Book Fund and the Canada Council for the Arts, and from the Province of British Columbia through the British Columbia Arts Council and the Book Publisher's Tax Credit.

This book has been produced on 100% post-consumer recycled, ancient-forest-free paper, processed chlorine-free and printed with vegetable-based dyes.

Printed and bound in Canada.

LIBRARY AND ARCHIVES CANADA CATALOGUING IN PUBLICATION

Hutchinson, Chris, 1972–
A brief history of the short-lived : poems / Chris Hutchinson.

ISBN 978-0-88971-266-9

I. Title.

PS8615.U823B75 2012   C811'.6   C2012-901363-3

For Meghan Martin

CONTENTS

THE GIFT

The spring malingers. He is sick of it—
This loose fabric of rain, all warp and no weft.
America, once predatory, has presumably fled.
It is hard to concentrate, to derive any prospects or
Feelings from this daguerreotype landscape. His eyes
Are the half-closed eyes of a nursing infant.
In each pupil a monitor glows, twin stars gone
Milky, nebular. Hunger and thirst
Sucked from the flesh, reborn to the markets
Are values of the purely abstract.
With the tip of his necktie he writes his name and
Bank account passwords onto the fogged window glass
And laughs. Something feline raises its head
From the void at his feet. It yawns
Showing the pink of its mouth like a baby's
Unclenching fist. He can't decide what
To call it, this living page from a book of pre-
Christian myths, this gracile creature with
Hawk's curved beak, ears elongated and feathered
And the burning blue wings it unfolds with a sound
Of wind-kindled leaves. His own name
Blurring, drips onto the windowsill where it
Puddles, and puzzles him, and exists there
Perfectly without him.

He sinks into the centre of his art, mischievous as a whirlpool.
The year is 1864. The Kingdom of Heavenly Peace has appeared
And disappeared, the peasants having died from eating
Toadstools as their children milked the blood of goats.
How he glides beneath the last proscenium, martinis twirling
In each hand. The year is 1977 and wistful Bucharest
Once again, is off the map. He drops his wand and
Flicks his tongue into her distant sex. Not the space
Beside the chest, but behind the silver-gilt ciborium
Is where a single shaft of sunlight bursts a mote of dust
From its penumbral ennui. The year is 1667. Milton
Is impoverished. *Paradise Lost* has been ransomed
For resurrected sight. Who wouldn't sell his soul to look at will
Through every pore? Why do felons reveal the subtlest of clues
In order to confess? He patrols the vespers, the gloaming and
The Middle Ages without a cigarette, guide or point of reference.
When we see him next we'll know how long it takes the breeze
To shimmy and to shape itself anew. The hour here is
11:41 am. The new Prime Minister has just collapsed
Into our Father's arms. Experimental surgeries to save his heart
Will soon become the final decadence in a land attuned
To making love as a private form of tyranny. Before computers
Time was not a river, just the caressing of the impermanence
Of truth: *et in arcadia ego!* His spree is over, his wallet empty
But for modern forgeries of ancient counterfeits. So tired and
Longing to escape the storms and voguish cycles of our lives
He hides amongst the Brotherhood of Sleeping Car Porters
Dozes off between the rats and saints.

REPRESENTATIONAL

These clothes don't just say "I'm clothes" they say "I'm fashion!"
~Tim Gunn

***

See? A new coat of paint
makes the insides glow:

what peers out from within
the silky brochure

for a Palm Beach
golf resort:

everyone's smile
says *I'm famous,*

and their eyes
never close.

DEATH OF THE INSTITUTIONAL ANALYSIS

A room inside a document.
Each desk with its decorative candy bowl
Its invisible lines of demarcation.
Glossy tiles meet the walls which
Contradict the nostalgic scent of
Ammonia mixed with pencil shavings.
There are no doors within perpetual light
And silence where these lines might serve
As an oblique reminder of occluded
Corridors. Though there have been tales
Of a stranger who claimed to hear
A buzzing sound beneath the floor. This was prior
To the renovations and the flow
Of a synthetic oxygen equivalent.
Now the ceilings rise towards transparency.
Everything's easy to know.

THE HISTORIOGRAPHER READS TO HER
TIME-TRAVELLING SON

On days best for bloodletting
Five sparrows will align
And pass like dark stars
Through Cassiopeia—this
According to the hermetic
Manuscript she is reading
To her son who is feverish and
Oblivious to the hour's irregular
Pulse. Through the window
He can almost see the horizon
Sloping, gently rolling
The moon across a frost-
Blighted field towards a fissure
In the cosmos. In this light
His mother explains the nacreous
Third eye of our amphibious past
Where even today we are held
By a darkness called *feeling*
A blindness called *thought.*
Will I become thoughtless
And bloodless as a Precambrian
Stone, or light as a sparrow
In preternatural flight?
Wonders the boy, still semi-
Awake in the suspended
Doubt of his mother's embrace—
Her fingertips, soft as leeches
Stroking his white face.

CROSSTOWN STILL LIFE

The future becomes past by way of the present
Reckons the thrift-store Poet Laureate whose next invention
Will be a weaponized word machine made from clerical errors.
Art is not the most evolved quadruped robot on earth
But it's close, clambering its way up the concrete steps despite
Random kicks from those religious officials grown jaundiced
Begrudging secular fads. The morning is sick with them and
With the yellow, orange and pink patchwork of its own complexion
Reflected in wave-furrows and oil sands—the morning becoming
Night by way of an afternoon everything's busy skyrocketing
Through: moorhens, Japanese paper, protractors, alphabets
Genome decoder rings and the missed phone calls from our dearly
Departed self-confidence. Never mind if our beliefs revolve
Around Calvary, the Smithsonian or *National Geographic*—
The body of Christ eaten by ants was not something anticipated by
The Immaculate Conception! "Is it our ethos in love with the figure
Crumbling in Rodin's earliest dream, or could it be that within all
Postures of stillness lurks a clandestine *What's next?*" asks our
Interlocutor, rattling his name like a curse as he cruises between cars
On the M train to Brooklyn. He is wearing a tan felt fedora
With an ostrich plume which bursts into flames the instant anyone
Drops a three-sided coin into his outstretched flipper.

NOT ODYSSEUS

The journey waylaid by feasting.
Tiny chimes of dust seasoning his tissues.

A shimmer of nerves and sexual exertion.
Symbolically the quince a stud horse grubs

Once the crickets have cursed the summer out
And unstitched each sequinned consonant

From its vowel. Going in circles... Quartz-white
Spray of white quartz, the masculine sailing fast and

Luminous beads of sweat materialize
As jellyfish on the underside of waves:

Windows within windows! His body
Not entering but falling through—

Not the vicissitudes of misfortune but
A sacrifice to the gods of

Shit-luck and
Historical revisionism.

CONSPIRACY TOURIST

The tenor of the report was such
You couldn't thread a speaker through the voice—

Something about each raindrop resembling a
Silver starlet suicide? It seemed

You'd picked the wrong hotel to
Give up daring the edge of artifice:

Above the traffic, lips poised
Over a steaming mug, you unleashed

Poseidon-tempests onto imagined
Fleets of innocents, flooded

The streets on a hydrophilic whim!
Then, years after your story was

Adapted for the screen,
You were half-unhinged by

Guilt, half by what they had
Conditioned you not to see—

But seeing it just the same.

REPRESENTATIONAL

With some effect we spoke our names, so there was, about our names, a certain presence.

***

It's cold. What exists
beyond sensory data?

My fictive part
of this story

the pen dissolving
upon contact with the page—

the page knowing nothing
of breath

or the immaterial
stuff of attention?

HAVING FALLEN THROUGH A DESCRIPTION

Next to twelve nights in Gibraltar
Your *sotto voce* come-hitherings
And this pseudo-avuncular
Faux-Parisian, would-be
Provocateur—I am far
Less melancholy in my
Horn-rimmed specs and my
Argyle sweater vest, but almost
As chemically unglued. Having
Fallen through a description
Wires from the sun respire
Like baby cobras
Libra is microwaveable while
Leo's chest regresses
To a pockmark. Another
Season in the dirt, wedged
Between crime scenes, these streets
Are neither whiskered nor wizened.
They are not furred, fuzzed or snow-blurred.
These streets are wind-confessing
Vestibules for rusted dreamboats
Regardless of our fenced-in and visibly
Androgynous sense of allure. Thus
The heart is sheer hearsay as its
Shrubs, stones and liquorice breath
Make several weak assertions.
For example: a bird's beak is a nib
Which plucks the *i*, and Tolstoy
Must not be forced to stoop inside
The bathysphere of our own

Delusions. So while Sisyphus
Dreams of carting a feather away
In a half-ton truck, we must seek
To ream the citrus from the fruit
Of our investments in conserving
Insurgent works of art. Whoops!
My blood just leapt from this
Rural ditch towards the theories
That ruined me, where two
Identical lions hunt the ranks
Of the pilgrims' stunned retreat.

ABOVE A GAMING HALL

Back then, you rarely slept.
In the gaming hall below, Dostoevsky
Crashed and pounded with a passion worthy
Of Beethoven's Fifth. Forget warmth. You crouched
Inside blizzards which seemed to draw force
From your poverty and self-estrangement. Nights
Held diversions, velleities, but no dreams.
Talks with ravens, imagined escapes from hospital gardens
Or visits to graveyards for the criminally insane would
Have to wait, as you rolled on bedsprings thrusting up
At angles wild as the surface of a crosswind sea.
Spent, you'd lose yourself inside the stained-glass panes
Above your writing desk, the haloed gaslights soft-
Focused to a candied mist. Was it a game, or pathetic
Romanticism, trying to envision the suffering of your life
As glass sifting separate colours from the light?
Recall the cold. How you'd tremble against
The mornings which seemed to hold fewer prospects
For celebrity than chances for a rendezvous
With the landlord's harelipped maid. Afterwards
You'd bathe in mildew and rotted gypsum or
Merge with shades of frankincense wafting in
From the Church of the Annunciation—giving a kiss
Of sweetness to the early hours. Often you'd weep
Loathing the frozen draughts, your own self-
Loathing, obliged to seek refuge within the favours
Of a jealous autocracy. From nothingness only
The shadows of words appeared like the wings of a bird
Lying frozen in banked snow. For years, you lingered
You survived the exhausted age by refusing

To rage or completely shatter. Must I remind you?
I am the voice you always knew but could never heed—
While in the rooms below, Dostoevsky's fits continued
His appetites increased, and by now his name
Has become legend beyond St. Petersburg.

THE INTELLECT WANTS TO DREAM

Listen, the intellect wants to dream—
Goes the tinny refrain of an ice-cream truck

Moving somewhere between
Unheard melodies and crass utterance.

Then a catastrophe of bells—children
Crashing into the senseless delight of themselves!

But what's sweeter is the loneliness
At the heart of every coupling

What's at risk—or so your mind insists
Like a hive of ionized honeybees.

Then your thought becomes a paper flower
Unfolded by an artless whim

And crumpled up by worrying neuroses
And planted in the heart of reason.

REPRESENTATIONAL

Impoverished yet contemplative, past generations once relied on pleasures transmitted through a landscape.

***

Above the tempest-
throes of a wind-

hectored fig limb
appears a crown

of lightning—
the artist's

gashed, exposed
canvas!

CAPTAIN NEMO RESURFACES

I wake up happy, then start to think.
A goddess enters with flippers and furious
Lips, reminding me of the play my Jungian
Analyst once forced me to see about the mimic
Octopus, *Changing in the Changes.*
Is it dawn already inside the world's
Subconscious, or is it still the postmodern
Age of aquatic mosaics where governments
Blur the edges of words? I feel the image
Of an actuary in swim trunks as I come
To the place where emotions collide with
Financial subsistence, where I am saving my
Breaths like those Atlantis-era modillions
Poseidon once salvaged and stuck beneath each
Roman cornice. At least that's what's reflected
In these ink blots of yours. And though I awoke
Buoyant and smiling like the pufferfish in some
Marine biologist's float parade, you'll see
I am glancing now above the crannied murk
At the media squinched unhappily
Into those trilobite faces we all know
From the pages of *American Scientist.* Ha!
Undersea fables are only half on my mind
While my genitals are packed so tightly inside
This wetsuit the colour of unrefined oil, providing
The cameras keep rolling and the trilobites swoon!
Yes, I've come back, despite my abhorrence of your
Deadening airs. I arise (each muscle, a swelling
Convex meniscus) not just from eddies
And swirls but from the eyes

Of tornadoes and hurricanes, from the mouths
Of rivers, deltas and alluvial fans—I've come
To spit poisonous pearls into your earth
Which rejects me and all of my people.

HENRY THE FORGOTTEN

After his snowdrops are trampled, Henry
The historian sulks, as though the air is wet
Cardboard he must punch through with an oddball wit he hasn't
The energy or keenness to produce. He feels like falling
Into an old Dutch painting where light rays pioneer a hornbeam
Countertop to chance the rim of a servant girl's lip.
But there are so many sharp memories he should soften
Then replicate, postcards he'll address to himself amid
The jade statues furred with dust, the bound-in-leather
Gilt-edged classics tumbling off imaginary
Shelves. Soon perhaps, he will be bitterly drunk
On whatever it is that ventures beyond his
Protestant past to become one in the crowd stepping
In time to the maniacal megaphone chants
Pierced by the protesting squelch of
Québécoise French. The truly faithless suddenly
Leaping out of themselves into daylight
·And springtime buds, and his fists sprouting
White knuckles. Everywhere the same pink
Squalling baby flashes its gleaming front teeth!
Is this the motherless infant he will become
Without a soothing voice, flattery or someone
To assure that all his technique has not been merely
To trace another civil account? Sulking
Behind a lead-paned window overlooking his
Minced garden and the paving stones where blue horses
Once drew carriages of tourists through a mélange
Of brick warehouses and across the cantilevered
Bridge—he wonders, was it ever his wish
To be adored for all his late-night revisions

Or to be torn from his childish fits like a page
From the book of Old Montreal?

LONG DISTANCE

Suddenly, remembering Saguaro Lake
Where the crowns of Palo Verde
Once swept beneath a gale like
Dishevelled loops of script—I need
To sit cross-legged, to lay my hands
Supine upon my thighs, to bow my head
Into my palms, to close my eyes and
Breathe. I must need more than this.
Somewhere I don't want to see, clouds
Become a backlit crystal display and those
Cursive trees, just countless arcs and
Strokes in one long, unsolvable
Equation. From this place—the desert
Crossed, the Rockies vaulted in the time
It takes a human being to gasp
For breath—*Are you listening?*—
The transmissions come, the storms
Of static. *Tell me*, I ask my friend
Who isn't here, *what use is waking*
To a phone inside a dream, or trying
To reach you through these disappearing
Lines of breath?

REPRESENTATIONAL

The future, undoubtedly, lies with the plot-less, actor-less form of exposition.
~ Sergei Eisenstein

***

The camera puts on its uniform.
Your eye salutes!
Then a whiteness
pervades everything.

Like the pinpoint of a simile
the actor once embodied a task
common to us both.

Cold fact: mimesis
makes money
make money.

But you wander off
into a blizzard's blank screen
away from the audience.

EQUINOX

One tree grows in the gated city
Like a leafy bulb screwed into the ground
Drawing the earth's current. No one notices.
Its green luminescence lives only in the minds
Of its inhabitant birds, sparrows and jays whose
Throats convert the tree's energy into a thrum
Of hallelujahs. Their praise spreads
Throughout the city, among impassive
Passersby, along stone and glass facades
And over traffic stalled at erotically exhausted
Cross-purposes. Still, no one seems to care.
Crowds assemble and disperse to a rhythm natural
To each initiate, every movement, well-moneyed
Perfectly rehearsed. While some might believe
In underground cults that summon the tides
They'll admit this to no one but themselves
In the mirror, after dark. Just as invisibly
Are the birds reabsorbed by the tree's conduit leaves
And offered up as budding white filaments reaching
For the winter sun's deracinated fire.
But few will acknowledge this overcast sky
Is uprooted depth. Who remembers whether
Certain days of the year once opened and closed
Like valves of the heart. Was this before
Or after the tree plunged its blind taproot down
Through the electrified soil and everyone fell
Light-headed, asleep? In the centre now
There's a sanctuary no one can see:
A self-enclosed poetics: a twofold dream.

SERIALIST

The self is no mystery, the mystery is
That there is something for us to stand on.
    ~George Oppen, "World, World—"

I.

Echoing rings of self-
location—

the poet
likes girls

the poet
likes boys

the poet
enjoys

idolizes idiots
worships the woeful—

II.

What it thinks
it is

leaning with
the dead weight

of its skeleton
pettifogging

radiance
a handprint

on glass.

III.

In the forsaken
illuminated manuscript
the owl's chest is white

as the smoke it thinks
might arise from a particle
physicist's pipe—

IV.

Its body could have been
stepson to empiricism
or a bright, malodorous liquid

said the hairless contortionist
as she bent the horizon blue
before it snapped black.

Its beauty is hidden

where that which is not seen anymore
is not to be spoken of
or even imagined.

v.

Rorschach blots
Freudian lips

tongues like flapping
prescription slips—

Should its serotonin be amplified
its spirit kept alive

as a simpering screw-up?
An olive-eyed innocent?

VI.

Because its love letters
are bordered by Victorian scrollwork
but smeared by what
heterogeneity has done
to its calligraphy hand

it wants to bulldoze
a kissing booth.

VII.

Without tracing the roots
of opposing points of view
amid a variable wood

the upshot of the law and
the celebrities it was warned about are
nearly sinister enough to beguile—

Hey, artistic insurgence!

VIII.

Successfully losing—

the sun clenched shut
like the Rose of Jericho,

black armbands boasting
the bright tragedies to come.

Splayed toes
transforming feet
into storm drains—finally

from the source of affliction to have
shaped something.

IX.

To free itself
a candle melts

into daemonic
female shapes

as a pinned eel
scribbles
its sensory data

where a coiled fist
minerals across
the reflective surface

of a cloud
in a parallel universe.

x.

Whoever corroborates the story
of a contemplative life
widens the spell
of its bedlam-eye.

Right here, amongst the perishable—
the glittering apparatus of youth!

The years it wants to curse
will be continued.

XI.

Uncomfortable
with prolonged

hugs
its smile

freezes, time
stretched taut—

caught between

tunnelling
its way

out of debt
or turning

to the criminal
mist.

XII.

Verbs bending around
the telekinetic presence
of money.

Hands, not knowing what to do.
Feet, a mimicry of chance.

Wine, a view through cracked amethyst?

Its eyelashes are the wires
of a marionette!

To push things further:
a visage

implant.

XIII.

Skies it thinks
with stars
drilled above
deep waters
never
end—

Nor do ordinary lives
frittered away
as winding
tributaries—

only to flourish
in the wilds, in a flash
of distraction!

XIV.

Soft-spoken syllables
evaporate
to sweet vapour.

Rhetoric is big business
as Byzantine networks
replace its circle of friends.

Each inner pendulum
pitched into flatspin—

xv.

Words
are cloudshapes
in the reflecting pool:

secure:
some artists
like men

demure:
some artists
like women

grandeur:
some artists
determine—

XVI.

Soon, the other half
of this conversation will

bow down
with the downtrodden

folding within another
gravel-coloured winter

an innocence
called *shame.*

XVII.

Gently it manages
to tip the lion's cage over
the embankment

of a promise
to drink only beer and wine
reclusively.

XVIII.

Its voice
surreptitiously
illumined—

thirst making birdsong
sweeter than hunger
makes inwardness
bitter—

while the late autumn fruit
is falling in love with
falling in love with
absolute silence.

XIX.

Green eyes gone
phosphorescent, guttering from
lack of oxygen—

Its friend's
suicide turned into a
balloon parade.

Pain, not
a container for lies
not a conduit
not a reason.

xx.

Pruning roses and
ironic expression—to add
by cutting away.

Each thorn, more obvious
in the vacant spaces.

Each finger blossoms.

TITIVILLUS

Soon, he thinks, he should find the room
From where, occasionally, beautiful voices can be heard.
But first he has to climb a flight of stairs, he must
Reach the floor where words are manufactured
From liquid-hot lead. Journeymen whose long-
Stemmed pipes fume beards of smoke tell him
With scalded eyes what he's already told himself
Though he hasn't understood. Already, the lines
Of his brow have darkened into a tortuous
Relief—not a map revealing some deep
Paternal instinct, but the spidery sketch of a child
Fathered by wind. Or so he sees himself
Reflected, as a giant silkworm moth batters itself
Against the window's glass, wanting in—each eye
He notes, like a tiny inkwell with feathery quill!
Perhaps there is no sanctuary, no secret
Guild—only rafters where, inside dense immobile
Shadows, he imagines the egg sacs of insects quietly
Bloom. The firebrick walls give heat, though his skin
Goose-fleshes at the pneumatic hiss and incessant clanging
From what appears, spot-lit at the centre of the room
To be a pair of steel wings buckled to a bench and
Beating out a panicked tattoo. He is afraid, but calm
Locked in the teeth of this new fascination. There is
No moth, no unmeasured expanse, only endless
Figures to be cast from the white-hearted lead.

LEGION

In service to the people, pressing my ear against the wall
I think I hear the poor scarabs trapped in amber celluloid.
This is after the uprising, but before the arrival
Of warships, and the wolf-like helicopters come
To *gawp-gawp-gawp*. In this room there are
Other rooms with walls made of yellow dust lit
By glowing screens. The doors are voices, all of them
Locked. In service to the people, lead reporters
Are sacking museums and on my orders they will escort
The mummified dead back to their network executives.
Only one throat can trumpet through these ancient gramophones.
Only my song can pierce the galvanized hummingbird's skull.
In the street there is smoke, human forms, shapes of blue
Twisted metal and police. What I say makes history
Obsolete. Like Herodotus on stilts I seek that white-haired
Raconteur who once swam with sharks and swallowed African
Hornets on a dare. Where is he now? Probably weeping in some
Sunset Strip hotel, his pinpoint oxford shirt spangled
With the blood of the silenced. In my absence, silence
Is my legion in service to the people.

POET IN MIDDLE AMERICA

As we read these lines, Lorca drives
Into the creature-stew of the valley's smog
Where palmettos with squid-like hats
Stand swarming the desert's shoulders.
His authentic self, pitted against the half-dead
Towns, hounds him as the sun atrophies
Into foothills. See the spark inside the chamber leap
An aeon's sleep as prehistoric matter resurrected
Growls to charge the far horizon. His eyes—drawn
To diamond junctions, tricked by folding and
Unfolding clovers, vexed as a scorpion's love
For butterflies—his sunburned eyes unreel
To chase hieratic scripts blazed in neon across
Embankments, culverts, and the concrete walls built
To screen frontage roads and crumbling neighbourhoods
From off-ramps and soaring interchanges—built to subdue
Revolt. Today the expressway is a flume of fire-
Reflecting steel. You say the twentieth century
Has been replaced and miles of earth skinned
Like ripened fruit. But let's recall the artist, alone
Yet not alone, speeding towards his unborn
Admirers: those of us in this desert who know his heart
Was filled with butterflies and bullets.

THE PARANOID ALGORITHM

In the end, there was the code, which demanded
A glamorous correlative, like breakdancing.
Just as personal misery absolved artistic pain, so it snowed
Methamphetamine in the Germanic forests of antiquity.
Freud took a little libation, wrenched out its little tongue.
God, we gave thanks for the fabric softener's anti-static properties
While you cursed its ubiquitous perfumes, went at it
Hammer and tongs. We should have thrown pineapples
Instead of grenades. Even our bombs might have learned to read.
Remember, our faces were once clean maps of the world
With the advent of the internet and the blurring of our Empire
Into a centre-less corporate state—this was before a microbe's
Breath caused a galactic cataclysm. So foretold
The cuneiform tablet, from the beginning.

REPRESENTATIONAL

Letters sprouted from our eyes, an unfolding of local rumours, and of perspectives smitten with the plains.

***

Under glass
the cracked porcelain

of a dragonfly's
wing decorates

the face of each
postage stamp.

CANADIAN PSYCHO

In the rear-view mirror
My home appeared no more
Than the world's tiniest stage
Where rose-coloured curtains soon fell
On a landscape of wooden courtesy.
Done flirting with Darwinian
Themes of survival in poetry
I believed in the debt my spirit
Could pay for public strength—
This I thought would make me
American. Gawd was I dumb!
Thanks to a feminist, I matured
Into the role of the oppressor
I abhorred. All the cocaine
And her adamantine Marxism made
Everything seem less Orwellian
And more like a bad flashback
To the historical *year* 1984.
When I awoke I discovered
My identity had been concocted
By something other than me.
Trapped in an upscale-hipster
Disney version of Bohemia
I could almost feel whatever
It was I thought they were
Going to allow me to become—
A wooden figurine? A tourist
Without a GPS? In the end
I settled for a self-projected
Figment of Paul Newman's

Ghost, who lit a stagey cigarette
Then hitchhiked north, alone—

COMMITTEE REPORT

~after Adrienne Rich

Being alive today is the same
As being alive yesterday—
Though our wisdom has dissolved
The gods which once held us hostage
And replaced them with new powers
To save us from questioning
Ourselves. Observe the self-loving
Sentence, which scholars claim has
Hoodwinked the young—how it preens
Licking its fur into conical swirls
Before stretching itself out to dry
In the sun. And while its syntax
Resembles our executive director's
Ginger moustache, let's not neglect
Its velveteen gloss, or the harpsichord
Strains of its genderless heart.
And when sorrow and cold come
To each *pied-à-terre*, and our French
Accents fall into shameful disuse, and when
The myth of poverty's charm gives itself over
To foment revolt—I predict nothing
Will happen, I foresee a tranquil end.
Conditions are perfect. Our logic
Not only beautiful, gently precludes
Anyone treacherous from speaking
(Or thinking the word!) *truth*.
But since we must justify our ways
Without explaining the system, let's say

Crafty confections make our prisons
Easier to hide: a fence in winter the sun
Flickers through, or the keys a pianist's
Hand stumbles down in a drunken attempt
At bravura—such iterations are the only
Art forms we will finance or publicly
Support! And while some of you worry
The malfunctions we praise as ironic
Evasions might soon be detected, exposing
Our guilt, please note how easy it is
To retreat inside the artifice of a self-
Contained wit. Colleagues, fear not.
At the pinnacle of success, work
Is pure service without the need
To question or describe the nature
Of the very thing we find ourselves
Most driven to pursue. Who would ever
Believe our metaphors speak only
For themselves? I predict, tomorrow
Scores of *artistes* will line up and beg
To decorate our eardrums with glissandos
And our dinner table with fashionable trinkets.

BEFORE THE WARS

From behind the bowls of flame-
Coloured apples, we watch soldiers
Return as nomads—nails bitten to half moons
Faces flattened with what happens
When a single memory holds intuition
By the throat. The service is terrible, our waitress
Bellicose. Because paying for bayonets to sprout
From the tip of each dull syllable feels
Worse than the night the café burned
And our plastic curios were all satanically
Transmogrified, we excuse ourselves
To the Everglades, abandon our children
To the atavistic tide. Yet this story is a trick
Of vision, swinging on a hinge like
That paper clip our analyst once used to fix
His fashionable glasses. We go back
To the year thermal lifts gave the dirigibles
The power to burst the hearts of all citizens
Born in exiguous rooms—brighter than clouds
Those airships were cocoon sacs
Of the lower heavens. Then hope turned to delirium
Tremens, just as a gold-toothed theosophist
Stumbled on crayfish shells in the cloistral bays
Of the afterlife. Slanting his brow
To the swallows darting like needle and thread
Along the treetops, living on apples and
Spitting out seeds like the dark eyes of birds
He was once our image of sweetness
And light—before the wars
Removed all traces of his name.

REPRESENTATIONAL

It is easy to be beautiful; it is difficult to appear so.
~ Frank O'Hara

***

In the fun-struck nation
you celebrate each new mood
with a Gauloises Light!

Lachrymose, self-conscious
without knowing why
you flex one eyebrow

but not for us.
Peacetime can be
monotonous without

round-trip cab fare
or the quixotic patter
of hawkers and cons—

those whose days are spent
lacing one voice through
a tortuous series

of disguises.

LENIN, AS I DESCEND

What appears as the cracked blade of a trowel
Is really a metropolis tilting its shoulders to the sea. Distance
Makes luxury yachts look the same as large cresting waves.
I am coming from where the snow line in spring recedes
Back into cloud. I am tumbling down. More than people there is
Evidence of people, recurring steel corners and curves
And silvered glass like a kind of piety locked
In granite. I am landing outside a row of neon-lit hotels
Where rain has built its chain-link fence around everything
That glows, where some unacknowledged firebrand
Has written *No Wars No Walls* across a wall
Of brick. Look, next week Elvis heads will be on sale
Beside the methadone clinic! It's true I could identify
And describe six more bogus signs of the apocalypse
If I weren't sinking through the pavement into the oily
Soil where the monolith of your brow is buried
With all the approbations of your wars written
In looping barbwire scripts and threaded red
With roses. Once, I wore my shirt buttoned
To my beard like you, but I've since lost patience
With my own impatience and the endless sales
Of your remaindered books. Please ignore
This sickle-shaped tattoo woven beneath the hairs
Above my heart—just tell me how the hell to drag
The suburbs down, once I'm Commissar
Of the Underground.

125

It's not the rate of recurrence that defines us—
This I explain at the symposium, passing around my modernist egg

While the wind kicks the building so cruelly my animus
Cracks open and bleeds through my shirt. I will need a tray

Of living specimens now to support my exegesis
Some organic prototypes unmutilated by the digital frontier.

Though my feelings are at stake more than my thesis—
My tears weeping tears, gaudy as the hall's chandelier.

I should curse my recursiveness!—my prismatic past
Drained to shades of grey. But after dark, when the hotel

Ignites and the flames are multiplying spires of brass
I will surely rise from such fashionable hell

Up through the residue of a century's sleep
Where the angels of technology await me.

EAST–WEST

Luxury secretes poverty away
Within the hollow pillars of its velvet drapes.
The director here wants an establishing shot
Of a copper-plated eagle's head, not an ironic
Lemon twist. Once the site of temporal displacement
Delphi has been retrofitted with a waterworks
And crowded with public officials ready to drag you
Through an umbra of gin and clove cigarettes.
These markets are unsafe. Each day splits
The difference between a first-class harvest
And a lousy one, the fear of crocodiles in the water
And of executives in office towers along
The Atlantic coast. You spend the spring
In dusty Tripoli, searching for arguments to justify
All points of view. Your breath ascends
A fog of a cerebral stylishness, then turns
To baroque landscapes which hide the razed
And blackened hills of your furtive, hell-bound years.
In a daze, the director has lost his footing
On an icy precipice. Below, the invaders' flagships
Have been set alight by a Phoenician god
Whose accomplishments include the pillaging
Of lakeshore villages where your own children
Pick through mounds of garbage in search of food.
From where you stand, you can almost
See the florid waste, the pigeon-mind
Of the starving.

THE PERSISTENCE OF SYCORAX

From what she has read, and from how she thinks
About the world, she conjures a galleon fleet rolling

On vast swells, masts slow-motion scrawling
Ciphers onto the sky's frayed parchment.

From all she has seen, she knows
To extract the angelic, white-gold speck

Of plutonium from crusts of her own
Dried blood, and when to unzip

The atomic nucleus. Her guardian spirit
Cares how she feels—that electromagnetic

Imposter, Setebos who once bribed
The mooncalf with counterfeit notes.

Lichens ice the edge of her scrolls.
The eye of her navel twines

With serpents. With all she has gleaned
She can prove evolution is

Timed to explode. We care little
About why or whom—burn her pages.

Which is how her knowledge ascends
On ladders of smoke.

AVATAR

Beneath a scapular brow he opens
The mouth of his eyes. We think anything is
Possible on the corner of Hope and Despair
Where sunlight spins silver from smog
And the Procrustean decree that all facial hair
Must function at the level of metonymy
Is embraced, even by the tourists.
Storefront windows depict in reverse
Cherry trees with their little burst fireworks
Of early spring. Such invisible powers are
Visible here: the dialectic between legislated
And jerry-built methods, and the centre lane
Like a calcified spine which divides the blameless
From the sick and the dead. Politically, your foam-
Mesh hat's on crooked, my plaid collar's popped.
Hence we read the fingers of his toes as hungrier
Than the holes in his skin, while his sneakers
We imagine are listening to those underground
Voices fake-coughing to themselves and echoing
Our thoughts about how we might embolden
Our position as pushers of compassion torqued
By the popular song: "Ode to the Crepuscular!"
No, I won't apologize for my prosthetic aesthetics.
No sooner do these trees ignite than they throw
Down their small picket signs and start to riot—
In celebration! Or so the scar beneath his lip
Whispers in a language that hasn't been translated
But will be soon, to be published in a book, thus
Legitimizing our careers.

REPRESENTATIONAL

> *The view is magnificent... all around a vast mountain chain of roofs studded*
> *with chimneys and attic windows like castles and ruins... and the sky so close*
> *– it is unrivalled.*
>   ~Carl Spitzweg

***

After illness, what hopeless love
begins to copy the works
of every Flemish master?

In truth, the spirit dwells in a loft
crawling with primeval silverfish
windows worming with drizzle.

In your lesser works, context
is a fringe of erasure, like dreams
that don't come true—

or a kind of suffering
that wriggles out from behind
the images when the images

are moved.

WET FEATHERS

In the dense summer heat and chlorine sting
From an upwind blaze, this city feels submerged—
The near distance, a smudged light my eye brushes past
Almost contemptuously, in some kind of rush.
Clouds cluster, barnacle-like above museums
And bookshops, then later in undulant rows that
Shadow the dotted lines of streetlights and cars.
Imagine a monastic apartment and a grotto-dim window
With a view of a tree branch bobbing like a skeletal fish
Not to the breeze but in time to the Mozart concerto
Floating in from the adjacent cafe. Self-conscious
In his velveteen fez, the owner envies his patrons
Unslipping the knots of each other's lives
While he grinds espresso into his nails, one finger
Bruised from repeatedly banging out filters.
"This world of ours," his friend Paris insists
"Is full of pretty girls, don't make my mistake!"
"And listen, the sound of rain is a tin man
Being nitpicked to death," I throw in before
I pay up and split, knowing a layer of ether hangs
Between the ceiling and the linoleum counters
Covering the tables' rotted-out wood. It is the same
Soft membrane of radiant malice I pass through when
Talking to someone without catching their eye
When speaking so awkwardly my syllables
Clank like the tuna-fish tin this little winged
Cat starts to lick the moment I sink into
Sleep. On waking, the skies have cleared
And the yellow sand is unwritten upon
Egyptian papyrus. In the distance, that beacon

The Library of Alexandria still stands!
"Ode to the wet-feathered dawn," burbles
Another would-be narrator in the ecstasy
Of drowning. Picture the fire in his mind haloed
By a fine-veiled mist. He is slipping
Through the waves. His body is writhing
Through a series of failed plots—

THE VALE OF TEMPE, AZ

Praise the Salt River, its blazon of industry:
Cross-hatched erosions, erasures, and the air

Gravity-structured, plumb lines describing where
Horizon meets fact, where plazas, palm trees

And interstate loops, framed and exalted
In steel by machines made to kill time

Furnish the glut and seal up the sky's
Impossibly sun-hammered vault—

Or so the disciple of progress will posit
Just as a train's ethereal shriek is warped

In velocity's wake. So in scorched
Mica-flecked rubble like pulverized logic

In Apollo's detritus, history either
Bent or distorted, we worship the fire.

FLYING DREAM, TERMINAL CITY

Lawns and boulevards have been painted
With the glow of crushed stars.
Every green tendril and blade frosted over
Curls tightly and shines. The sidewalks
Once dotted with cigarettes before everyone quit
Once covered in dimes like first spots of rain
Soon stream with humans.
On telephone poles ravens play totem
For the weed-softened tourists.
Cravat-sporting twins, *enfants terribles* shriek
Murder crossing the red. Rush-hour traffic clots
And unclots. Buses grunt and sigh and mimic
Our distress, knowing we are gone before
We arrive, knowing on waking we must try
To rephrase what yesterday we failed to express.
Now is the time. We are falling through silence
And open like snowflakes unfolding
Insensible scripts. Anything is possible
Notwithstanding these barricades
And cavalcades of mounted police.
We escape to the rooftops where the sky
Is eclipsed by a billboard which would have us
Mortgage our lives to a humanoid duck.
There are rules to flying, even in dreams.
At the base of the blue mountain
Above a bride's veil of fog, an eagle
Wheels on a wing tip
And drops.

THE OTHER BARON OF WILLIAMSBURG, NY

De-friended by the sanctimonious spare-parts aficionado
His life is a thesis statement on power-save mode.
He starts his journey in poverty and ends with Venetian masks
Prosaically littering the cloister's necropolis—
Just another visa overstayer in the Empire State.
Deer in tube socks embolden the tapestry
Like a deep meditation experience on steroids.
The water in his glass lying awake all night
Staring at the ceiling, thinking
Language is the lens that blurs
These forms of feeling. A palliative carnation
He blesses the meadow with his clover scent.
He reads your relaxation journal and becomes distressed.
"Whoever kills God invents Irony"—so says
His lovely protégé, whose "Cat in Love with an Owl" video
Went viral the same year she missed the boat
To her high school reunion in Hoboken, NJ. She told him twice
"The night sky looks like it lost a fight with a porcupine"
And he looked, without really listening.

REPRESENTATIONAL

We must wash literature off ourselves. We want to be men above all,
to be human.
    ~Antonin Artaud

***

Off fighting your weaknesses
you forgot your strengths.

There are times when being human
is the last refuge for those

with no other excuse.
Should this man-made century

envelop your body
like a chrysalis?

Form, you might say
is a species of nostalgia.

But you're never home.
You're a statue

in the asylum.
Holding your left shoe

you died alone.

IMAGO

I got tired of the image of my tribe
and moved out.
　　~Tomaž Šalamun

CHAPTER I

Dear wasted youth: there are holes inside the
sky, crows of missing time.

***

In the wrong city, in the wrong hands, a gun
holds its breath, wanting to believe in the
corporeal nature of some imminent threat.

***

From my last affair, for you, the undressed, I
shall fashion the autumnal cloak of allure all
mothers fear their sons slipping into!

CHAPTER II

While waiting for someone to invent the machine that will challenge your lack of initiative, consider, if you care to stay awhile, why technology exists.

***

Caught and twisted in a cypress branch, the plastic grocery bag of the heart asks, "Where did my aura go? Who locked the door outside the consumerist universe?"

***

It was likely the underground chemist I know, who is also a novelist and close in appearance but opposite in temperament to a guy I once danced with, a Marxist drifter who was a lousy dresser but as happy as a full-time drunk could get.

***

Mine, the only childhood so buoyantly shrugging off each reprimand with its hollow shoulder, its crayon-scrawled grin.

CHAPTER III

Please remove this shrapnel from my chest—you French philosophers who keep misconstruing my shoelaces as tripwires.

***

Carefree is a suburb of Phoenix, according to the textbook salesman, whose daughter will train to become dental hygienist, even though we all believe in her ability to churn out middling works of art.

***

Beneath the stairs, a fledgling philanthropist is about to write, "Where does origination come from?" but curls up into a ball instead.

CHAPTER IV

While it's true that all perspectives are essentially the same, each one unfolds, petal-like, separately.

***

Unlike the orange arch we passed beneath, holding hands and crouching low, not wanting to obscure the scene, the painted lagoon we discovered, the one you were sure concealed the shipwreck of my youth, glowed a lurid green.

***

O how your current living situation, open to the soft sense domesticity makes as it reasons against the bar scene, prevents you from drinking straight from the carton of milk!

CHAPTER V

The lime pit's already dug for our next
political letdown.

***

Notice the arbours' vine-riddled latticework
where lozenges of sun kiss the graves of your
eyes.

***

In the hotel lobby of the dispossessed, to see
the fountain as a chandelier, try standing on
your head.

***

This room has all the charm of a wasp's
nest on fire. Tourist that I am—perpetually
passing through.

***

Last night I vomited in the ashtray. I saran-
wrapped the moon.

CHAPTER IX

Above the snow leopard, an apparition of Luxembourg appears—the joyful apotheosis of a career?

***

Hey you, whose mothers possess a killing insouciance, I'd like to offer your fathers each a peppermint!

***

Sure, they wrote her scenes in black and white, in the back alleys of syntax, in the boroughs of bad grammar. No, I won't give you an example.

CHAPTER VI

Stuck in your throat is every church bell
which rusted before it could sing—

***

Come talk to me, she said at the prenatal
class reunion, when you're ready to shut up.

***

In the orchestra pit of my argument it
seemed as if the kettledrum player was either
brainless or drunk.

***

How drizzle's denizens once believed in
night-rainbows, but not in the benevolent
intentions of mist.

***

Naturally I was there, after the accident,
along with a dawn's chorus of robins,
worshipping in the aftermath.

CHAPTER VII

The least hasty among us swung in on the hinge of a fly's wing—said the small fire reflected in your wineglass full of water.

***

Eventually, each manufactured object will spill beyond the perimeters of its function.

***

My wicker chair, a repository for cat urine and russet-coloured leaves.

***

It's true: another celebrity sex tape on the loose means more than all the oceans' undiscovered mountains and valleys.

CHAPTER VIII

As she jumped the turnstile, she winked!
New York was like that—according to the
umpire bent over his letterpress like a
dyslexic prince.

***

That morning we tidied up, then hijacked
innocence for more sleep. Only the pilot light
kept its lonely vigil.

***

How our look-alikes, having traded
extravagant gifts, loosened the turnbuckle of
their scruples—

***

I was orphaned by an untied shoelace. You
were found throwing vinegar into the eyes
of lions.

CHAPTER X

The failed chess player who breathes an oath between a glistening pair of legs, or the strip mall in its indefatigable emptiness—which does the metaphor prefer?

***

I've thrown my self-portrait into the dumpster, along with my career in self-portraiture. Thus the cricket in my cupboard consumes one teaspoon of silence at a time.

***

Vintage is another term for threadbare. To which shall we defer?

***

Each night, behind the video arcade, the funambulist, presumably alone, practises in the nude.

CHAPTER XI

OK, I'll admit, my neighbour's genius is like an origami crane, unfolding—so why does she keep whispering to her foxtail hat?

***

Deep down we're all superficial, have the same idea which is to have no ideas, spend whole days just trying to wake up, dressed in seasonal thrift in a town with no wonder, weather or style.

***

Crossed swords bar the entranceway to the gallery suite—as in the fine-tuning of authority to scientific points.

***

The way our daughter on a swing once swooped with chain-link wings, turned the sky upside down. Today her raiment is drab as a chimney sweep's.

CHAPTER XII

Dawn writes her cover letter, acquitting the usual suspects.

***

On the east side of town they'll be cleaning the pools for the water polo tournament. In the west, citizenship shall no longer be mandatory for those with an unfaltering stroke.

***

But now, let's see who trips to vault the fence, who slips into oblivion at the first touch of frost on the leaves of wild carrot.

***

It's a new day in the mechanical reproduction of famous watercolours—it's the age of the Monet calendar.

CHAPTER XIII

Write anywhere, except amongst the stains
and odours beneath the sink. During the day,
fruit flies punctuate the unfinished dishes.

***

At night, two wolves patrol the dream world,
eyes the colour of pissed-on snow.

***

Fair maiden, after all those cigars at the May
Day Parade, why did your henchman spit on
my eel-skin boots?

***

If California represents how we commonly
construe the octopus as purple and skittish—
then what?

***

Then I'll polish my faith to the sheen of a new
cellular phone.

CHAPTER XIV

After peeling the decals from your bike and sticking them to your forehead, you wheel around the circus elephant.

***

Whatever the reason—at the grocery store a child screams herself into existence beneath a stand of lifestyle magazines.

***

A physician holds a lighter so that the flame licks around the rim, then presses the searing metal to his forearm like a syringe.

***

Pain unbuckles its belt. Its corpulence spills out in waves.

CHAPTER XV

"Look," she said because she was fond of emphasis, "I was here before gentrification, before that belligerent waiter, the one with the lazy eye, went searching for recovery groups in the she-male district of the Lower East Side."

***

Thus began your karmic unravelling—the day you refused to see us at the retirement home due to the perpetual outbreak of World War II.

***

Forever alone, the novelist announces to his imaginary guests that he will soon set the tableaux for a figurative dinner.

***

Psst. The moon is a gate that only appears to open and close.

Thanks to the Impressionists, I'm allergic to women and cinquefoils.

***

Perhaps paper sun hats will grow wings if the makers of tricycles try harder to renounce the colour red.

***

No Mr. Soul Taker, Stravinsky never lived here.

In a state of contingency, there is at least one stable variable. So the weatherman thought, before pulling the trigger.

***

Those specks swarming my vision weren't worth mentioning—until my optometrist decided to run for office.

***

I miss my old neighbourhood, my restive self. Who *wasn't* from Malta back then? Who didn't wear an eye patch, or own a bloodthirsty hawk?

***

Today the coltish tips of pampas grass whipping the air is a kind of eroticism that bores you.

CHAPTER XVIII

Even as the trees stop talking and begin to howl, still your face will not vanish from the clouds.

***

He got sick of saying he was happy, as in many ways he was very sad—so he began describing how sad he was, believing in this way happiness might come to him.

***

Whoever heard of a brownfield mirage? Hunched on the horizon, each building is the coffee-stained filter of a crumpled cigarette.

***

I confess, my accomplishments once appeared reflected in a hubcap rolling beneath the viaduct from a flaming interstate wreck.

I imagined I could imagine all the doors of all your houses opening and closing like the valves of some sad musical instrument. But I was mistaken.

VIEW FROM A FLAG

I'm on the roof, looking down.
Although the night is old, I've never been more awake
To visions and sounds. A furnace kicks against the wall.
Beneath the floor, children whisper. They are growing
Ponderously fat with sleep. A thread of milky light will split
Their mother's abdomen, a spark will wink, as the moving
Moment fans the rebel-cackle of the flames. I do no more
Than just repeat, I remind myself that images are images
Of images whose fountain source is dry as history's
Old ink. Soon this night will open, newly chaste.
I'll unfold and watch the children scatter from the blaze
Through bars of angry light and across the cold
Obscurely starlit fields.

ACKNOWLEDGEMENTS

For those who had a hand in shaping this collection, I am grateful. To my friends and allies, I'd like to apologize, and give thanks.

Credit is also due to the editors who published earlier versions of certain poems in the following magazines and journals: *Arc Magazine, Canadian Literature, Event, Malahat Review, Ryga Journal, sub-TERRAIN, Vallum.*

This book could not have been written without the support of the Canada Council for the Arts. Thanks for the grant.

ABOUT THE AUTHOR

Chris Hutchinson is the author of *Unfamiliar Weather* (Muses' Company, 2005) and *Other People's Lives* (Brick Books, 2009). His work has been translated into Chinese and has appeared in numerous Canadian and US literary journals and anthologies. Born in Montreal and raised on Vancouver Island, he has pursued various livelihoods in Vancouver, Dawson City, Edmonton, Nelson, Kelowna, Phoenix and Brooklyn, cooking in restaurants or occasionally teaching creative writing at high schools, colleges and universities. He hasn't been home in years.